DYBBOOKS

The first months leading up to a marriage can be so full of joy, anticipation, and excitement that many people don't take the time to really get to know their partner. They might not realize how different they are until after the ring has been placed on their finger. This is why asking your future partner the right questions are so vital for couples who want a healthy marriage because that gives both partners an opportunity to talk about everything.

These questions reveal expectations and concerns and help each person understand the needs and hopes of their loved one. A perfect resource for churches, counselors, dating couples, and young men and women who dream of a forever marriage.

This book covers questions about these topics:

Questions about Communication
Questions about Family
Questions about Lifestyle
Questions about Sex
Questions about Work and career
Questions about Entertainment
Questions about Finance Management
Questions about Managing conflicts
Questions about Religion and spirituality
Questions about Health
Extra questions

Family

1   Before you get married, do you want to have a prenuptial contract? Why yes, or why not?

2   Are you close to your family?

3   Have you ever been estranged from your family?

4   How often would you like to visit your family?

5   How often will your partner's family visit you?

6   Do you have a family history of disease or genetic abnormalities?

7   Do you get along with your family?

8   Do you value the opinions of your parents or extended family?

9   Do you think your partner's family is too intrusive?

10   Do you think it's important that you and your partner have a good relationship with each other's families?

11   Do you have a family history of genetic diseases or abnormalities?

12   What if one of your family members said they don't love your partner?

13   Did you need to break up with someone because of family feuds?

14   How would you handle family visits on vacation?

15   When making an important decision, do you feel the need to consult with your partner first?

16   Have unresolved or ongoing family problems ever been a reason for a relationship to break up?

17   If your partner's parents got sick, would you mind taking them in?

18   Do you think some of your fears, worries, or otherwise mental health are affected by something which happened in your childhood?

19   What's the most hurtful thing your parents ever said to you?

20   How often would you like to visit your partner's family?

21   Does it matter if your family likes your partner?

22   Did your parents fight a lot? How do they settle a dispute? Do you think you act in the same way?

23   Do your parents still have influence over your decisions?

Communication

1   Does your partner ever resent you?

2   Do you think that you find fault with your partner?

3   Did your partner disappoint you? Did he hurt you?

4   How does your partner communicate their love for you?

5   How does your partner make you feel safe and accepted?

6   what's the most effective way to get your attention?

7   How much time do you spend on the phone every day?

8   Do you have an unlisted phone number? If yes, why?

9   How do you feel when your partner disagrees with you?

10   Does it ever seem to you that your partner criticizes you?

11   How do you feel about sharing your feelings with your partner?

12   How do you feel when your partner

disagree with you?

13   What do you admire about the way your mother and father treat each other?

14   How do you deal with your partner when he is upset?

15   Are you willing to tell your partner if you have a problem?

16   Would you tell your partner a white lie to avoid hurting my feelings?

17   Do you think your partner nagging too much?

18   Have your partner ever disappointed you or caused you pain?

19   Do you consider yourself a communicator or a private person?

20   In what circumstances would you not answer the phone?

21   Has communication ever been a reason to break up a relationship?

22   Do you consider your disputes so far with your partner resolved or are they still affecting your relationship?

23   Are yu willing to tell your partner when you are stressed?

24   What would you do to make your partner smile?

25   Was there ever something you didn't want to tell your partner?

26   What is the best way to communicate difficult feelings to yourself without taking offense?

27   How will we work things out without getting into combat?

28   Do you ever fear that your partner will judge you?

29   Has your partner ever kept secrets from you?

30   Do you have trust issues with your partner?

31   What can make you not want to talk to your partner?

32   What kind of discuss you always want to have with your partner?

33   What happens after you and your

partner argue?

34   Does your partner have problems with apologizing?

35   Do you think you will be able to communicate with your partner in any circumstance and on any subject?

Lifestyle

1   Where does you prefer to live?

2   What is your relationship to tobacco, drugs and drinking?

3   How will we divide the responsibilities?

4   What kind of house do you want to live in? -house, apartment, etc.-

5   Are you an hintroverted or an extroverted person?

6   Do you agree to hire an assistant, use cleaning?

7   How do you feel about your partner's standards of cleanliness and tidiness?

8   How much time will you expect to spend your partner?

9   What is your idea of a fair division of labor in your home?

10   Do you prefer urban or rural areas?

11   How much money do you need to live the lifestyle you want?

12   Do you consider yourself a calm

person, or are you more of the determined type?

13   What do you like to do after work?

14   How much money you like to spend or save?

15   How important is exercise in your life?

16   How many hours of sleep do you need each night?

17   Do do you like to sleed your weekends?

18   What do you think of my lonely friends? Would you be okay if I party with them once in a while?

19   Who will shop and cook in our relationship?

20   How often do you plan to eat out? What restaurants do you like the most?

21   Does you like to cook or order?

22   Do you like to be showered and dressed in clean clothes every day, even on weekends or vacations?

23   How many trips you prefer to take with your partner ?

24   Do you prefer to live in the city, the countryside, or on the beach? Why?

25   What does your perfect day off look like?

26   How often do you like to go to parties?

27   Are you handy with tools and power tools, or do you rely on professional services?

28   What does your ideal vacation look like?

29   What is your idea of perfect relaxation?

30   Has having a car or a house or something material ever been a reason to break up in a relationship?

31   Are you a physically affectionate person?

32   If you'd suddenly be outrageously rich, would you significantly change

your life? If yes, how would you change it?

33   What is your favorite season of the year?

34   Do you prefer being awake during the day or the night?

35   How would you fairly assign household chores?

Sex

1   Do you feel comfortable taking the initiative when having sex? If yes, why? If not, why?

2   What are your sex expectations?

3   Is there something missing in your sexual relationship?

4   Will you tell me if you are not sexually satisfied?

5   What do you need to get ready for sex?

6   Do you think the physical component in this relationship will be enough for you?

7   Will you openly bring up your crush on someone (if it happens) before something significant happens "on the side"?

8   How would you handle it if your sex life got boring?

9   What are your expectations regarding sex?

10   Are you comfortable talking openly about sex? If not, why's that?

11   Have you ever doubted your sexuality?

12   Is sexual fidelity a primary condition in a good marriage?

13   What do you like best about sex?

14   Are you usually in the mood for sex?

15   Do you use sex as an outlet? If something bothers you, do you use sex to try to help him feel better?

16   How many times yu wanna have sex with your partner?

17   What attracts and excites you the most?

18   Is sex for you a method to relieve stress?

19   Have you ever used sex previously to appease your partner or avoid a topic?

20   Do you and youprioritize sex?

21   Do you think you can trust me enough to discuss our sexual differences, fears, or fantasies?

22   Is there anything unusual I should

know about?

23   What kind of sex you like to have?

24   What is your favorite sex position?

25   Have you ever broken up with a partner because of bad sex?

26   Do you agree to give up the things you feel attracted to you outside of our relationship before something meaning-ful develops?

27   Is you open with your partner in terms of sex?

28   What is the ideal period for sex?

Work
and
career

1   Are you working on what you wanted?

2   How supportive are you of your partner's career goals?

3   What are your career goals?

4   Where do you see your career in 10 years?

5   How much time do your spend at work?

6   How many hours a week do you work?

7   How passionate are you about your career?

8   What does your job entail? (For example, travel, work from home, dangerous tasks...)

9   What if your partner can't stand his professional situation and need a break?

10   What is your dream job?

11   Do you think work-life balance may put a strain on your relationship with your partner?

12   Are you a workaholic?

13   Do you prioritize work over other aspects of your life?

14   Are you always looking forward to learning something new?

15   What do consider most : your profession or yur passion?

16   What are your professional aspirations?

17   What is your retirement plan? What do you intend to do when you stop working?

18   What to do if your partner cannot find a job for a long time or he needs a "professional" break?

19   What are your career goals for the near and far future?

20   Have you ever been fired?

21   Would you mind moving if your partner had to move for his job?

22   What would you like to do when you are retired?

23   Have you ever suddenly left a job? Have you ever changed jobs?

24   Would you understand if your partner worked overtime for extended periods of time?

25   Do you consider your job a career or just a job?

26   If your partner is offered a dream job in another part of the country, are you ready to move?

27   Has your job ever been a reason to break up a relationship?

28   What's your education level? Are you proud about it? Do you want to increase it?

Entertainment

1   Do you like to travel?

2   Where you want to travel?

3   How does an ideal day look like for you?

4   How much are you willing to spend for a vacation?

5   During the holidays, do you visit your family, stay with friends, or enjoy time to yourself?

6   What's one passion that makes happy?

7   How often do you want to travel?

8   How much would you say you spend on leisure activities weekly?

9   Where would you like to travel?

10 D you like drinking or going to strip clubs...?

11 Have significantly different hobbies caused you to break up in the past?

12 How important is alone time to you?

13 What do you think of my going on a trip with the girls (boys) for a few weeks?

14 How important is spending time with friends to you?

15 What would the perfect weekend evening be for you?

Finance Management

1   How much money do you earn?

2   What are all your current personal debts?

3   Would you be willing to get a second job if we had financial problems?

4   Do you get stressed when faced with financial problems? How do you deal with stress?

5   What do you think about borrowing money?

6   Who will take care of the financial affairs of the house?

7   Do you want to be rich? How important is money for you?

8   Are we going to have a budget?

9   Who will pay the bills?

10   Do you believe in establishing a family budget?

11   Are you more thrifty or wasteful?

12   Are we going to save money as a priority?

13   How well do you create your bud-

gets?

14   Do we sign a pre-wedding certificate before the wedding?

15   Do you feel comfortable budgeting together for our married life?

16   Who will take care of household financial matters?

17   Would you want us to set a specific amount we're willing to spend every month?

18   Would you be ok with just you being employed from the two of us?

19   What is your opinion on how to spend money?

20   What if we both wanted something but couldn't afford both?

21   Do you think saving for retirement is important?

22   Was money a big part of your previous relationships? Did you pay for everything? Or, did your partner pay for everything?

23   Are you good with handling finances like tax? Which one of us would be doing the math?

24   How will we manage finances - expenses after the wedding?

25   Do you prefer separate bank accounts or assets in different names? Why?

26   Do you have any debt? If yes, how are you solving it?

27   Would you like to split all the money with your partner or split the money into different accounts?

28   How do you feel about spending money?

29   How do you feel about helping me pay off my debts?

30   Do you have any other financial obligations to another person for legal or moral reasons that I should be aware of?

31   Do you think it's important to save for retirement?

32   How often do you use credit cards, and what do you buy with them?

33   How should we prepare for a finan-cial emergency?

34   What are your feelings about saving money?

35   Would you be willing to get a second job if we had financial problems?

36   What justifies the debt?

37   What is financially important to you - having a house, a nice car, a business, expensive clothes, travel?

38   What is more important to you, the size of the house - flat or its location?

39   What is your opinion on how to save money?

40   Are you planning to buy a house - flat or rent?

41   Has money ever been used as a means of control in your past relation-ships, by either side? Did you break up because of money?

Manage
conflicts

1   Can you come up with an example of a conflict we had that you think we have resolved?

2   Would you be willing to go to marriage counseling if we had marital problems?

3   What would be unacceptable in the event of a dispute?

4   If there is a disagreement between me and your family, which side do you choose?

5   How do you handle disagreements?

6   How did your family deal with conflicts while you were growing up?

7   How do you usually express your anger?

8   How could you communicate that you are not sexually satisfied?

9   What is your conflict style (compromise, confrontational - avoidant, adaptable...)?

10   What's the best way to handle dis-

agreements in a marriage?

11   How do you behave during a conflict?

12   How can I better communicate with
you?

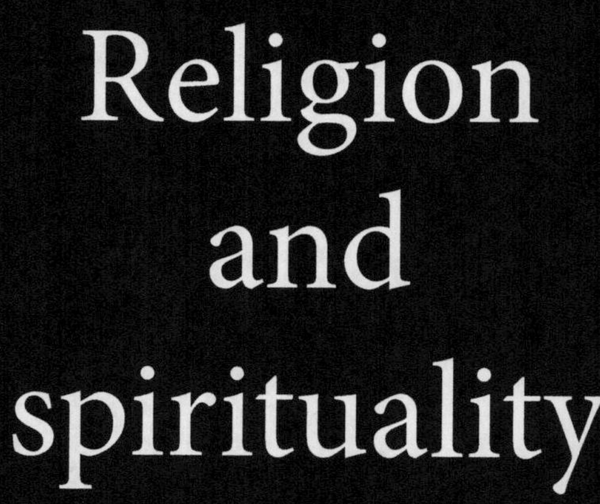

Religion
and
spirituality

1	Do you make life decisions based on your religious belief?

2	Do you regularly go to a place of worship?

3	What are your spiritual or religious beliefs?

4	Do you believe in God? What does this mean for you?

5	Do you engage in spiritual practices outside of religion?

6	Is it a problem if you have different political ideals than your partner?

7	Is it important that you and your partner share the same religious beliefs?

8	Is it important to you that your children are educated in your religion?

9	Is it a problem if you have different spiritual beliefs than your partner?

10	Do you have a religion? Is it an important part of your life?

11	Is spirituality a part of your daily and practical life?

12   Do you pray or engage in certain spiritual activities regularly?

13   Do you consider yourself a religious person? A spiritual person?

14   Does you expect your partner to participate in your religion?

15   How important is it for you to observe a spiritual or religious practice?

16   How involved are you in your spiritual or religious community?

17   Who are the most important people for you?

18   Do you believe in life after death?

19   Does your religion impose any behavioral restrictions (diet, clothes, social, finance, lifestyle...) that could affect your partner?

20   Has religion or spiritual practice ever been a reason for the breakup of a relationship?

21   What expectations do you have regarding the involvement of your partner

in your spiritual or religious activities?

22   Do you expect your children to be raised in a particular spiritual or religious faith, and if so, what would that look like?

Health

1   What can you say about your current state of health?

2   How do you feel about our full physical examination before marriage?

3   Are there serious illnesses in your
family: genetic, mental disorders,

4   Have you ever had a serious illness
or a surgery?

5   Do you think taking care of yourself,
and your physical and mental health is
critical?

6   Are there any genetic disorders in
your family or a history of cancer, heart
disease, or chronic illness?

7   Would you object to mental health
treatment?

8   Do you have any kind of allergic?

9   If your had to change his diet because of medical issues, would you be
willing to change yours?

10   Are you willing to exercise with your
partner to improve our health?

11   Do you have health insurance?

12   How do you feel about vaccinations?

13   Have you ever suffered from an eating disorder?

14   Do you take any kind of medication?

15   Have you ever been treated for a mental disorder?

16   Do you have any kind of addiction?

17   Do you like sports? Which ones? Do you want to practice something with your partner?

18   Were you ever hospitalized? If so, what for?

19   Do you have any conditions which can be a daily problem, like gastrointestinal problems?

20   Did you ever break up with someone, or has anyone broken up with you because of health-related issues?

21   Do you have any health problems which interfere with your sex life?

22   Do you have medical insurance and

dental insurance?

23   Have you ever been in a physically or emotionally abusive relationship?

24   Is exercise a regular activity for you? Are you looking to make it part of your day?

25   Do you follow a diet or some guidelines, or do you just eat whatever, whenever?

26   Do you have any habits like smoking or drinking? If yes, how often? Is it affecting your health? How much money do you spend on such habits?

27   Do you have a medical problem that affects your ability to have a satisfying sex life?

Extra
questions

1	What kind of boks you like to read, what kind of movies music you like ?

2	Where do you get your news

3	Do you believe what you read and see on the news, or do you question where the information is coming from?

4	Do you maintain a family tradition around certain holidays?

5	How important are birthday parties to you?

6	Do you have a car? If not, do you think about having one?

7	Does popular culture have a major impact on your life?

8	What is your favorite style of music?

9	Do you have fun with your partner's closest friends?

10	What kind of fashiom style you have?

11	Have you ever lost a friendship be-cause of a relationship? Has any friend-ship ever been a reason to break up a relationship?

12   Do you prefer having a close relationship with your neighbors?

13   How would you rate the priorities in
your life: partner, school, friends, hobbies, work, family, ?

14   Do you prefer a continuous work
schedule or flexible schedules?

15   Let's suppose you are experiencing
problems in your marriage, Who will
you seek help from?

16   How can you support your partner's
hobbies?

17   Is there anything you would regret
not being able to do or achieve if you
married your partner?

18   Are you a physically affectionate
person?

19   What is your favorite season of the
year?

20   What makes you really angry? What
do you do when you're really angry?

21   What makes you happiest? What do you do when you're happy?

22   Is it a problem if you have to work with members of multiple ethnicities, cultures, and beliefs?

23   What would be your reaction if your child dated someone of another nationality, ethnicity, or political views?

24   When you are in a bad mood, how should your partner treat you?

25   What are your views on having a pet?

26   If your partner had a pet, would you be willing to care for it even though you didn't like it?

27   Are you into pop culture?

28   How often do you meet up with your friends? Do you talk regularly? Text or over the phone?

29   Do you have a close friend of the opposite sex? Would it be a problem if your partner has one?

30   What comes first: friends or your romantic relationship?

31   Have you ever refused to help a friend in need? If so, why?

32   Is music a big part of your life, or do you rarely listen to it? What's your favorite genre?

33   Is a pet just a domesticated animal, or a family member?

34   Do you try and block time for involvement in your local community?

35   What do you fear?

36   Is there anyone close to you who feels we shouldn't get married? Why? Should we talk about this?

37   Do you have any racial prejudice?

38   Were you raised in a family with traditional values?

39   Is it important to have a space of your own at home?

40   Is accumulating money important to you?

41   Do you believe in prenuptial agreements?

42   What's your opinion of racism?

43   Would you sacrifice some of your own happiness & financial security in order to help somebody else?

44   Are you willing to respect another person's culture and traditions even if you don't agree with them?

45   Is it a problem if you have to work with members of multiple ethnicities, cultures, and beliefs?

46   Were you ever robbed or otherwise the victim of a violent crime?

47   Has your home ever been broken into? Did you move afterward or do you still live there?

48   Are you a righteous person?

49   Is strong physical attraction a necessity for you to connect deeply with your partner?

50   Do you wish to always be viewed as

attractive?

51   How long does it take you to get over an insult?

52   Are women simply better at household chores like changing a baby's diaper? Should only men know how to handle a hammer?

53   What do you think of social media?

54   D you you like dogs or a cats?

55   How do you celebrate when something important happens?

56   What is your biggest limitation?

57   What kind of TV shows do you like to watch?

58   What's the best gift your partner has ever given you?

59   Do you consider yourself a law-abiding person? Have you ever been arrested? If yes, why?

60   Have you ever been in jail? If yes, why?

61 Do you collaborate with your local

community on projects for homeless people or other disfavoured groups?

62 Do you make an effort to keep your apartment block tidied up?

63 Overall, would you say you're law-abiding?

64 What would be your reaction if your child dated someone of another nationality, ethnicity, or political views?

65 Have you had to break up with previous partners because of different views on race, ethnicity, culture or other associated concepts?

66 Are there people whose opinions you really don't value at all?

67 Do you generally feel self-assured? Are you willing to have a go at things you're not that skilled at - yet -?

68 Is there something, in particular, you dislike about yourself? Physical or otherwise.

69 Have you ever been charged for a

crime?

70   What is your greatest strength?

71   Would you consider plastic surgery to "fix" something which you view as an imperfection?

72   Do you use make-up? How much? How often? How long does it take you to apply it? How much money do you spend on it?

73   Would you become angry or dissatisfied if I gained a noticeable amount of weight?

74   Are you really in touch with fashion? How much do you spend on clothes?

75   Have you ever donated to a charity? What kind?

76   Would you volunteer for a cause you believe in?

77   Are you quick to judge people?

78   What could your partner do in the future that arouses your distrust?

79   Would you feel comfortable trans-

ferring all your money into your partner's bank account?

80   Are you sure you'll keep trust in
your partner no matter what?

81   Have there been times when you
were not comfortable with the way your
partner behaved with the opposite sex?
If so, when and what did he do?

82   Could your difference with your
partner be a source of conflict in the future?

83   Is there something about marriage
that scares you?

84   What makes you most insecure?
How do you deal with your insecurities?

85   What makes you more secure?

86   Which holidays do you believe are
the most important to celebrate?

87   What kind of food you like to eat?

88   What kind of hobbies you have?

89   Do you have a dog, cat, or other pet?

90   Do you believe that a person should

give up their pet if it gets in the way of the relationship?

91 Do you consider your pets to be members of your family?

92 Is it important for you to be involved with your local community?

93 Are women simply better at household chores like changing a baby's diaper? Should only men know how to handle a hammer?

94 Have you had to break up with previous partners because of different views on race, ethnicity, culture or other associated concepts?

95 What makes you afraid?

96 What kills your joy and passion?

97 What makes you smile in difficult times?

98 What makes you feel most alive?

99 Would you say you have a best friend or multiple best friends? How did you meet? What do you appreciate most

about them?

100 Do you believe that a certain amount of money should be set aside for pleasure, even if you are on a tight budget?

101 Has financial condition ever been a reason to break up a relationship?

102 Is it important to you that your partner accepts and likes your friends?

103 Is it important for you and your partner to have mutual friends?

104 Do you make new friends easily?

105 What's the longest relationship you've ever had? Why did it end, and what lesson did you learn?

106 Have you ever sought marriage counseling? What did the experience teach you?

107 How important is it for you to always look your best?

108 How important is your partner look?

109 Do you worry about getting old? Do

you worry about losing your looks?

110 If a friend needs you, can they count on your support?

111 Do you often participate in community projects?

112 Do you think it's important to contribute your time or money to charity?

113 What kind of charities would you like to support? Do you make any kind of donation? Which one?

114 Have you ever served in the military?

115 Are there household responsibilities that you believe are the exclusive domain of a man or a woman? Why do you believe this?

116 Do you believe that marriages are stronger if the wife leaves most decisions to her husband?

117 How important is equality in marriage? Define what you mean by equality.

118 Do you believe that roles in your

family should be filled by the person best equipped for the job, even if it's an unconventional arrangement?

119 Do you like going to concerts?

120 Do you enjoy going to museums or art exhibitions?

121 Do you like to dance?

122 Do you like to watch TV?

123 Is there a time of year when you are more involved in activities like football, basketball, or other sports?

124 Is it important for you to attend social events regularly, or rarely?

125 Do you go out at least one night a week, or do you prefer to have fun at home?

126 Do you consider yourself a good driver?

127 Do you like to cook? What kind of food you like to eat?

128 Does your work environment discriminate against any ethnicity?

129 Do you have a fine appreciation for food, or is it more like "fuel" for you to get through the day?

130 Do you make time to eat at a table, or are you always in a rush?

131 Are you a good cook? If not, do you expect your partner to cook?

132 Is it a necessity that you eat with your partner?

133 How would you feel if your child was dating someone of another race or ethnicity? The same sex? How would you feel if he or she married this person?

134 Are you aware of your own racial and ethnic prejudices? Which ones are they? Where do they come from?

135 Has having different ethnicities ever been a source of tension and stress for you in any relationship?

136 What were your family views on race, ethnicity, and differences?

137 Is it important to you that your part-

ner shares your views on race, ethnicity, and differences?

9 798848 017984